THE FROGS

Aristoph

AUTHORED by Kristen Osborne-Bartucca
UPDATED AND REVISED by Aaron Suduiko

COVER DESIGN by Table XI Partners LLC
COVER PHOTO by Olivia Verma and © 2005 GradeSaver, LLC

BOOK DESIGN by Table XI Partners LLC

Published by GradeSaver LLC, www.gradesaver.com

First published in the United States of America by GradeSaver LLC. 2015

ISBN 978-1-60259-525-5

Printed in the United States of America

For other products and additional information please visit http://www.gradesaver.com

Table of Contents

Biography of Aristophanes (450 BCE–388 BCE)

Aristophanes is considered the most accomplished of the Greek comic poets, and his place in the Western canon is immovable. His surviving eleven plays are mainstays of the stage, scholarly discourse, and literature and theatre courses in colleges and universities.

Aristophanes was born around 450 BC to Phillippus and Zenodora. He was from the deme of Cydathenaeum, born in Attica near Athens. There is very little known about his life; what scholars have gleaned comes from his work and the writing of other poets and philosopher. Plato portrayed him as a raucous man in his *Symposium*, and he has been celebrated for his keen, biting wit and satire, as well as for his intellectual prowess.

Aristophanes grew up in a time of immense Athenian power, prosperity, and artistic achievement. The Peloponnesian War between Athens and Sparta, which began in 431 BCE and lasted for about 25 years, profoundly affected him. As Harold Bloom wrote, "the spirit of his work reflects both the former predominance and later reestablishment of Athens. On the one hand, his work is an expression of freedom and exuberance, of democratic and cultural self-confidence...on the other hand, his work also reflects a time in which Athens' self-confidence is being tested and threatened with enormous conflict." He often used actual people and events in his works, and was renowned for his social and political commentary. His work is also highly crass and even obscene in terms of its humor centered on sex and bodily functions.

Many of his plays are examples of Old Comedy, while others near the end of his life are classified as Middle Comedy. His first play (now lost) was *The Banqueters*, written in 427 BCE. *Babylonians*, from 426 BCE, caused controversy at the Great Dionysia (an annual festival to honor Dionysus), when the demagogue Cleon criticized Aristophanes for lampooning the city's magistrates before foreigners. Although Athenians enjoyed freedom of speech, Aristophanes was indeed often the target of hostility on behalf of politicians. Never daunted, Aristophanes' two plays, *The Acharnians* and *Knights*, satirized the situation with Cleon and resulted in prizes for the poet.

Clouds (423 BCE) and *Wasps* (422 BCE) showed Aristophanes at the height of his talent, as he brings intellectuals, educators, Socrates, and the Athenian jury system under his microscope. He is justly lauded for *Birds* (414 BCE), a fantastical utopian play that probes the current state of affairs in Athens. Other plays also dealt with the political situation in Athens; the famed *Lysistrata* (411 BCE) featured the women of Sparta and Athens using sex to preclude their husbands from participating in the war. *Frogs* (405 BCE) concerns poetry, along with Aristophanes' belief that the deceased poet Euripides was more talented than anyone living at the time. After several decades of awards and success, Aristophanes was renowned enough to play around with the structures of drama, and was thus celebrated for his improvisations and innovations.

Aristophanes died around 388 BCE. While 11 plays survive, there are about 32 lost to history, and many surviving fragments and citations.

The Frogs Study Guide

Frogs, or *The Frogs*, is one of Aristophanes's greatest comedies and is justly celebrated for its wit and keen commentary on Athenian politics and society. It is the last surviving work of Old Comedy and is thus also notable for its heralding a passing era of literature. While it is a comedy, it is also a trenchant political satire and expresses Aristophanes's views on Athenian democracy, the value of poetry, and the need for a return of traditional values.

Frogs won first place at the Lenaea, an annual Athenian dramatic festival and competition honoring Dionysus, beating Phrynichus's *Muses* and Platon's *Cleophon*. Uncommon for its time, it was awarded a second performance the following week for the strength of its parabasis. According to the ancient *Life of Aristophanes*, the poet was officially commended and given a wreath of sacred olive for the lines about the disenfranchised. He may have changed a few of the lines for the restaging. Philonides, a frequent producer of Aristophanes' plays, produced the play.

A precedent for the play is Eupolis's *Demoi*, which also featured the resurrection of deceased figures such as Solon, Aristides, and Pericles. It was written in a time of turmoil, as Athens was still at war with Sparta. An oligarchic revolution was replaced with democracy in 411 BCE. Two other events bore significance to the play: Alcibiades, the famed military commander, was sentenced to die in 415 BCE but escaped to the Spartan side, was taken back to Athens, and finally exiled in 406 BCE; and the battle of Arginusae in 406 saw the Athenians defeating the Spartans but finding it impossible to retrieve their comrades on ships wrecked by bad weather, and condemning the military commanders as a group to death. The themes of the decline of Athens and the decline of tragedy as a great form of art are thus intertwined.

The scholar Charles Paul Segal notes that the structure of the play is unique because the first half is a journey archetype, and the second half consists of the contest motif. The nature of Dionysus's evolution from a crass, jesting figure to a weighty arbiter of taste and the fate of Athens has also garnered a great deal of attention.

Scholars do their best to imagine what the play would have looked like performed in its own time. There is speculation as to whether or not the audience would have heard and seen the frogs, or merely heard them off-stage. Charon's boat may have been on wheels, and there may have been a real donkey or a "stick donkey," which would have added to the humorous aspect of Xanthias's complaints about the baggage.

Owing to its entrenched position in the Western canon, it is no wonder that *Frogs* has been referenced in literature, television, music, and other works of the theater. Most interestingly, the frogs' chant of "Brekekekéx-koáx-koáx" is part of Stanford University's rallying call.

The Frogs Summary

Frogs, or *The Frogs*, is one of Aristophanes's greatest comedies and is justly celebrated for its wit and keen commentary on Athenian politics and society. It is the last surviving work of Old Comedy and is thus also notable for heralding a passing era of literature. While it is a comedy, it is also a trenchant political satire and expresses Aristophanes's views on Athenian democracy, the value of poetry The play begins with Dionysus, dressed up as Heracles, and his servant Xanthias, riding a donkey, traveling to Heracles' house. Heracles is amused at Dionysus's costume. Dionysus asks him how they can get to the underworld to fetch the poet Euripides for Athens, and what sort of obstacles they might expect to encounter. Heracles provides them with information, and the travelers depart.

Dionysus is ferried across the lake by Charon, but Xanthias has to travel around because he is a slave. Along this journey, a chorus of frogs bursts out into song, annoying Dionysus. However, the god then joins in their boisterous song.

Dionysus and Xanthias join up on the other side of the lake, but before they can go very far they encounter the monster Empusa. Dionysus is extremely frightened and soils his clothing. The Chorus of Initiates, part of the Eleusinian Mysteries, enters and sings a song to Iacchus, Demeter, and her daughter Persephone.

Arriving at Pluto's house, Dionysus and Xanthias knock on the door. Thinking he is Heracles, the doorman, Aeacus, curses him. Dionysus tells Xanthias to wear his disguise, but asks for it back once a beautiful woman comes outside and invites "Heracles" to a banquet with other ladies. The innkeeper and Plathane come out and lambast the supposed Heracles as well, prompting Dionysus to once more give the costume back to Xanthias.

Aeacus returns and orders the seizure of Heracles for past his bad deeds. Xanthias-as-Heracles says Aeacus ought to torture his slave (Dionysus) to prove his own innocence. Eventually both claim to be gods, and Aeacus tortures both to see if this is true. Both Xanthias and Dionysus feel pain but pretend not to, as gods normally are not supposed to feel bodily pain. Finally, Aeacus says he will see if Pluto and Persephone will vouch for their divinity.

Inside, Aeacus talks to Xanthias about how Aeschylus and Euripides are fighting over who is the most accomplished tragic poet. Aeschylus already possesses the chair but Euripides is challenging him for it. Pluto calls a contest and Dionysus is made the judge. Both poets criticize each other, and then pray to their respective gods. The competition begins.

In a series of contests, Aeschylus and Euripides discuss who is better at prologues, lyrics, and making their audience better citizens. Euripides claims to have slimmed tragedy down from its ponderousness and made it more accessible to the common person. He also says Aeschylus is verbose. Aeschylus, for his part, criticizes the meter of Euripides' work and claims that his verse is wanton.

Dionysus cannot seem to come to a conclusion, so he orders the two poets' verses to be weighed. Because he refers to lofty things such as death and rivers, Aeschylus wins the weighing.

Finally, the two poets are asked to comment on how the Athenians should deal with the statesman Alcibiades. Dionysus decides Aeschylus is the overall winner, and he, the poet, and Pluto return to Pluto's house for a banquet. Aeschylus tells Pluto to give his chair to Socrates once he departs for the upper world. The chorus praises Aeschylus and proclaims that it hopes he will assist Athens with sound advice.

The Frogs Characters

Dionysus

The god of both wine and ecstatic mystical religion, Dionysus is the protagonist of the play, first seeking to travel to Hades to bring back a poet of wise counsel to help Athens, and then judging the poetic contest between Euripides and Aeschylus. He is cocky but cowardly, self-seeking and crass.

Xanthias

The keen-witted and ambitious slave of Dionysus, Xanthias likes to complain about and compete with his master.

Heracles

The famous son of Zeus who completed the Twelve Labors. Heracles in this play provides Dionysus with advice on traveling to the underworld. Heracles's past deeds there are vilified by Aeacus and the innkeepers.

Charon

The ferryman on the river Styx; in the play he takes Dionysus across the lake to Hades.

Aeacus

The doorman of Pluto's house in Hades; he hates Heracles for stealing Cerberus and thus tries to torture Dionysus and Xanthias when they are disguised as Heracles.

Maid of Persephone

Thinking Heracles has arrived at Pluto's house, she invites him in for Persephone's meal and dancing girls.

Innkeeper

The woman who runs the inn in Hades; he dislikes Heracles for his behavior on his visit there.

Plathane

Another female innkeeper in Hades who dislikes Heracles for his bad behavior when he traveled there.

Slave of Pluto

Speaks with Xanthias about how he criticizes his master behind his back, and gives information about the upcoming contest between Aeschylus and Euripides.

Pluto

The god of the underworld and husband of Persephone, Pluto calls the contest between poets and allows the winner to return to Athens.

Euripedes

The recently deceased poet whom Dionysus originally intends to bring back from the underworld. Euripides was a tragic poet who often wrote of the common people. Aeschylus criticizes him for wanton verse and witty but decadent intellectualism.

Aeschylus

The renowned tragic poet who engages in a contest with Euripides to see who holds the chair of honor next to Pluto. While Euripides mocks him as stentorian and verbose, Dionysus finds his verse more traditional, sagacious, and necessary to help Athens in their time of need, and thus brings him back to the world above.

Chorus of Frogs

Sings for Dionysus while he takes Charon's boat across the Styx, jesting and teasing with their rambunctious croaking and singing.

Chorus of Initiates

Part of the Eleusinian Mysteries, the Initiates help Dionysus and Xanthias on their path and also sing of the rites and members of the Mysteries, the glories of Demeter and Iacchus; they also poke fun at notable politicians and poets.

Persephone

The daughter of Demeter and the wife of Pluto.

The Frogs Glossary

blarney

nonsense-talk

brandishing

wielding

burgeoning

growing quickly

clamored

loudly called for

croquettes

a small often rounded mass consisting usually of minced meat, fish, or vegetable coated with egg and bread crumbs and deep-fried (source: m-w.com)

depilated

removed hair from

dillydallying

procrastinating

euphonious

pleasing to hear

factionalism

a situation in which small groups within larger groups (i.e., factions) seek their own interests

foments

causing something bad to happen, like a war or rebellion

forsworn

guilty of perjury

gullets

throats

hemlock

a type of plant; in this context, a poison derived from this plant

hirsute

hairy

lacerate

cut; shred

minestrone

an Italian soup made with vegetables and meat

parse

to examine in a close, detailed way

pungent

having a strong impression due to being clever

scion

descendent, heir

unalloyed

pure, unmixed

urbane

polite, sophisticated

The Frogs Themes

The value of poetry

Poetry does not exist simply to entertain; rather, according to Aristophanes, it can impart a moral message and instruct its listeners to be better citizens and human beings. The works of the great tragic poets live on (dramatized in the play by Aeschylus being brought back to life) and can shape the characters of Athenians. In their contest, Euripides and Aeschylus boast of their own verse and what it can do: Euripides claims he teaches people to think critically and rationally, and Aeschylus taught them to be bold and yearn to defeat their enemies. Furthermore, as Aeschylus narrates, the noble poets "revealed mystic rites to us", "gave us oracles and cures for diseases" and "good instruction / in tactics, virtues, and weaponry of men" (80). Poetry thus offers life lessons, and is not merely an art form.

The decline of Athens

Aristophanes wrote *Frogs* during a period of Athens's decline, and his play reflects such tensions. Athens was in the midst of the Peleponnesian War with Sparta, and faced a myriad of troubles with politicians and demagogues. The democracy faced internal and external troubles, and *Frogs* asserts Aristophanes's view that one of the ways to save it was to bring the poet Euripides (later Aeschylus) back from Hades to counsel the Athenians. Throughout the text Aristophanes attacks those who seek to harm Athens, those who put the wrong people in charge, those who are self-interested, and those who do not help morale. His anxiety for his city-state is apparent even amidst his keen lampooning of officials.

Identity

Identity is a major concern of the first part of the play, with a focus on costumes, disguise, misidentification, and concomitant confusion. It is used for humorous purposes and also offers insights into character and the play itself. Dionysus travels in the guise of Heracles, allowing him to ignore any associations with himself and to hopefully attain the same success as Heracles in his underworld tasks. He is keen to slough off the costume, though, and give it to Xanthias when it serves him. Dionysus's identity would have been quite obvious to contemporary viewers, but his attempt to don different disguises and flit between such disguises and his own identity serves to further the assertion that Dionysus has not yet come into his own in the first part of the play, and is on a journey to attain real authority. Aristophanes's focus on identity also allows the audience to grasp the nature of theater itself, as it is self-reflecting device.

Ambition

Several of the prominent figures in the play display a heightened sense of ambition. Dionysus and Xanthias butt heads as each tries to assert their dominance: Xanthias is trying to resist insubordination by his master, and Dionysus is trying to keep his slave in his place. The balance of power shifts frequently, destabilizing their identities. Aeschlyus and Euripides also seek to exercise their ambitions to be considered the foremost tragic poet, and engage in a lengthy and vitriolic contest. Their literary and political perspectives are put to the mettle, and the result of their clashing ambitions is a clear message regarding what Athens needs to regain its former glory: Aeschylus and his wise counsel. Ambition is thus not always negative, and can be illuminating.

Tradition and morality

While Dionysus originally intended to bring Euripides back with him from the underworld, he realizes that it would be far better for the city of Athens to have Aeschylus, whose works embody tradition and morality. The play espouses the idea that, while Euripides's works might be amusing or technically accomplished or clever, they will not suffice to retain order, good behavior, and procure stability in the demos. Aeschylus, on the other hand, offers intelligence and wisdom, and, as the Chorus says, can "grant fine idea that will bring fine blessings" (107). It is part of Dionysus's journey (both literal and intellectual) that he realizes that tradition and morality are virtues, particularly in a time of unrest.

Dionysus' evolution

Dionysus, unsurprisingly as the god of wine and mystical ecstasy, is a wild, energetic, and pleasure-seeking character. He is also crass, boastful, self-indulgent, and cowardly. Although he is wise enough to venture down into Hades for a poet, he does not yet know whom he needs. Along his journey he reveals his flaws and limitations, and is tested. He is chosen to judge the poets' contest and is thus given his own test: can he wisely arbitrate between Euripides and Aeschylus, and choose the one whose verse will help Athens out the most? Thankfully for Athens, Dionysus evolves and matures throughout this contest as he is forced to think deeply about Athens's needs. He chooses the poet that will be best for Athens, thus indicating that while he will no doubt always be a little uncouth and fanciful, he can also be perspicacious and wise.

The value of comedy

Aristophanes was a paragon of Old Comedic literature, keen-witted, clever, insightful, and masterful in his construction of humorous themes. In *Frogs* he makes a case for bringing back a great tragic poet to assist Athens, but, significantly, he does so through the lens of comedy. In this crass, sometimes silly, play, weighty themes are dealt with in a very effective manner. Aristophanes makes the case that comedy can also be a vehicle for truth and moral messages, that is does not have to simply be lighthearted entertainment.

The Frogs Quotes and Analysis

I need a talented poet, / 'for some are gone, and those that live are bad.'

Dionysus, 27

In this statement Dionysus encapsulates one of the major archetypes of the text -- the journey -- and one of its major themes -- Athens's need for a real poet to help them regain their former glory and power. Dionysus believes that a poet of Euripides's stature (he, of course, changes to Aeschylus, but the idea is the same) will help Athens, but that he must descend into Hades to find such a poet since everyone living today is, in Dionysus's damning words, "cast-offs and merely empty chatter, / choirs of swallows, wreckers of their art, / who maybe get a chorus and are soon forgotten, / after having a single piss upon Tragedy" (28). This is the bold and provocative Aristophanes speaking through his protagonist, identifying his peers as insipid and fame-hungry, aware that there are no "potent" poets left whose verse can inspire and instruct. The overall point of *Frogs* is that Aeschylus's words should be turned to in this time of need, as they offer wise counsel.

An ancient mariner will ferry you across / in a skiff no bigger than this, for a fare of two obols.

Heracles, 31

In Dionysus's journey, he has to cross over from one realm to the next, where he will encounter numerous obstacles and creatures both helpful and harmful. His passage in the rowboat with Charon, and his paying his fee, is his entry into the liminal space of the river Styx that takes him to Hades. Charon is a figure commonly known to students of Greek mythology, especially those who know of Heracles's journeys. Charon's job, according to the myths, was to ferry newly deceased souls across Styx and Acheron to Hades. He is often depicted as an old man, usually haggard, brusque and irritable in demeanor. His name means "of keen gaze," which is possibly a synonym for death. *Frogs* is filled with allusions to Greek mythology and the writing of the Greek comedians and tragedians; while it might take a modern reader a great deal of sifting through footnotes to illuminate all of the references, the contemporary viewer of the play would be conversant in all of the allusions.

Exalted Iacchus, inventor of most enjoyable / festive song, come and march along with us / to the goddess...

Chorus, 47

This quote is found in the part of the text that contains the Eleusinan Mysteries (see Additional Content). Here the chorus moves in their procession, carrying out their sacred rites and worshipping the goddess Demeter. They also evoke Iacchus, which is another name for Dionysus, and ask him to come with them to the goddess. In some Greek mythology, Dionysus was the son of Zeus and Demeter. He was commonly seen as the torchbearer in the procession from Eleusis. While this association was well known, in *Frogs* Dionysus's summoning by the Chorus of Initiates has almost a temptation-like quality to it. He needs to proceed along his way to procure Aeschylus, not dally in the fields with the revelers. He is attracted by their dance but continues to Pluto's door. This encounter between hero-journeyman and ethereal, mystical creatures of another world is a common motif in the journey archetype.

> *You're the very worst coward on heaven and earth!*
>
> *Xanthias, 51*

Dionysus is, without a doubt, a prideful, self-confident, and arrogant figure. He is a god, of course, but possesses all of the trappings of a self-centered human being afflicted with hubris and shortsightedness. He does anything that will bring him pleasure and avoids anything that is harmful, difficult, or dull. As with any hero (if one might call Dionysus that), he does indeed possess a large flaw: his cowardice. Xanthias comes right out here and says it, identifying his master's shortcoming for the audience. This comes after a particularly crass and humorous instance where Dionysus shits himself due to his fear of the Empusa. Dionysus has always been far from being a noble protagonist, but this is his nadir. It will take his arbitration in the contest between poets and his eventual wise choice to redeem him from his weak, cowardly nature.

> *And I'll make you a gentlemanly offer: / take my slave here and torture him, and if you catch me / in any wrongdoing, then take me and put me to death.*
>
> *Xanthias, 58*

This is a passage that might seem curious to modern readers, but it was a reality of ancient Greek life that would not have seemed strange at all to the audience of *Frogs*. Under Athenian law, slaves could not be witnesses in the courts unless the owner gave consent and the testimony was obtained under duress. The owner and the adversary would have previously agreed upon the conditions. The courts were not often apt to accept such offers by an owner and challenges by an adversary. And, as may be expected, citizens could not be tortured but as slaves were not citizens, they were fair game. What makes this scene amusing is the identity game played between Dionysus and Xanthias, and the subsequent torture in all of its buffoonery. Torture was rendered acceptable through the guise of comedy.

> *First, we think that all / the citizens should be made equal, and their fears removed...Next I say that no one in the city should be disenfranchised.*

Chorus Leader, 62

In 'parabasis', the Chorus steps away from the main action of the play and offers commentary on the political situation in Athens. It is very clear about what it wants to happen. In the first point, they say that all citizens should be equal and any fears of being prosecuted for any offenses they committed under the oligarchy of 411 should be removed (even though there was an amnesty in 410). It also does not want to see anyone lose their voice in the democracy, as well as a few other concerns. The parabasis is an important component of the text, for it articulates the concerns Aristophanes is dealing with thematically. Athens has and is experiencing a great deal of instability, politically and in terms of foreign policy. There are internal and external threats to the democracy, that sacred institution. It is unequivocally important that Athenian citizens do not see any erosion of their rights. Through poetry, Aristophanes is making a potent political statement.

Why, it's like nirvana / whenever I curse my master behind his back!

Slave to Pluto, 65

In this amusing interlude, Xanthias speaks with the slave of Pluto. The slave, gregarious and voluble, speaks of all the ways he tries to subvert his master's authority. He talks behind his back, mutters when he is beaten, meddles in his master's affairs, and eavesdrops and blabs about his findings to outsiders. The audience of *Frogs* would have recognized these acts of subversion problematic, but they certainly rang true. Xanthias spends his time acting in a similar fashion, revealing Aristophanes's keen understanding of the tense dynamic between masters and servants. Slavery was seen as natural in ancient Greece, and there were many levels of enslavement, but that did not preclude animosity or hostility on the part of both master and slave. Xanthias is a keen voice for the issues inherent in this practice.

But the poet has a special duty to conceal / what's wicked, / not to stage it or teach it.

Aeschylus, 82

Aeschylus and Euripides spend time discussing the value of poetry, and both have good points. Euripides explains that his verse helped people think rationally and organize their houses better, and that poetry "[turns] people into better / members of their communities" (79). Aeschylus muses on all the noble poets' ideas and contributions, especially those found in his own work. He says that a poet should make sure that what they are writing has a benefit to the people listening to it, for poetry is profoundly powerful and impactful, not merely entertainment. What is deleterious about Euripides's work is that he "taught people to chitchat and gab" (83) and featured women behaving badly. By contrast, Aeschylus's work is dignified and didactic, and that is why he is ultimately the winner of the contest.

I've had enough too; what I'd like to do is take him to the scales, / which is the only true test of our poetry; / the weight of our utterances will be the decisive proof.

Aeschylus, 97

Dionysus cannot seem to choose whose verses are better, so the poets turn to a weighing. This scene was no doubt modeled on Aeschylus's play, *Weighing of Souls*, where Zeus weighed the souls of Achilles and Memnon. This *pyschostasia* is also found in Homer and Egyptian mythology. Indeed, Aeschylus and Euripides both have their fates in the balance -who will win the Chair of Tragedy, and who will accompany Dionysus back to the living world? Aeschylus wins this contest because he speaks of weightier things, such as the river, Death, chariots, and corpses, while Euripides spoke of lighter topics. This is a commentary on the type of poetry that Aristophanes believed was necessary to help Athens regain its position of prominence -no mere cleverness or fluff or beguilement, but morality and tradition and seriousness.

It was my tongue that swore: I'm choosing Aeschylus.

Dionysus, 104

Dionysus initially descended to Hades to bring back Euripides, a poet he admired greatly. He even described his desire for Euripides as a "passion" and a "longing" (26). However, after a long series of contests, Dionysus chooses Aeschylus, the older and more traditional poet. He does this because he realizes that Athens does not need the clever wit and "slippery character" (27) of Euripides; rather, Athens needs a poet of wise counsel and intractable morality. Dionysus chooses Aeschylus because he has evolved and come to understand the true nature of tragic poetry and its capabilities. By Aristophanes having his protagonist make this choice, he is making a statement about what his city-state needs. It is unambiguous, and establishes Aristophanes as a rather conservative figure himself. His concern for Athens is also linked to his concern for the decline of tragedy; by pointing to Aeschylus as the winner, Aistophanes also suggests that poetry like Aeschylus's should be returned to.

The Frogs Scene I Summary and Analysis

Scene I

Dionysus and Xanthias enter. Dionysus is disguised as Hercules and Xanthias rides a donkey with the baggage. Xanthias suggests Dionysus say something amusing to make the audience laugh, and they joke about Xanthias shifting the baggage so he can relieve himself. Xanthias complains that he wants to do what others, like the playwrights Lycis and Ameipsias and Phrynichus can do –hump the baggage.

Dionysus scolds Xanthias for complaining, and they banter about whether the donkey or Xanthias is truly bearing the load of the baggage.

They arrive at the door. Dionysus tells Xanthias to dismount, and knocks. Heracles opens it, wondering who is banging so loudly. He sees Dionysus and begins to laugh, amused at the lion skin getup Dionysus is wearing. He asks Dionysus where he has been, and the latter says he was serving topside with Cleisthenes (the latter often teased for homosexuality). He says he then got a longing. Heracles teases him about this, but Dionysus tells him not to jest.

He says his longing is for Euripides, even though he is dead, and states that "Nobody on earth can persuade me not / to go after him." He plans to go down to Hades because he needs a talented poet; there is no one living that is good. He rejects Iophen because he is unsure, and Sophocles is too mild. Agathon, Xenocles, and Pythangelus are also inadequate.

In the meantime, Xanthias complains further about his shoulder. Heracles asks if there are other poets here that might suffice, but Dionysus rejects them as "cast-offs and merely empty chatter" (28). There are no "potent" poets left (28).

After some gentle ribbing, Dionysus tells Heracles he has come to figure out how to find the friends of his that time he went after Cerberus, and all the places to stay along the way. Despite Heracles's objections to his plan, Dionysus persists. Heracles begins to suggest options for death, offering up hanging and poison and jumping off a building. Dionysus rejects all these and says he plans to go the same way Heracles went.

Heracles tells him how to do it. First, he will come to a large lake and will be ferried across by a mariner. He will then see innumerable frightful beasts, then a river of flowing excrement, then people guilty of all manner of terrible things. Then he will hear pipes and see sunshine, and men and women will be there. They are the Initiates and will tell him everything he needs to know.

Pleased, Dionysus tells Xanthias to get the baggage again and prepare to go. Pallbearers and a corpse enter. Dionysus asks if they want to haul bags to Hades, and one asks how much they will be paid. They cannot agree on a sum, and Dionysus curses him.

Charon rows his boat over and he and Dionysus greet each other. Charon asks where they are going, and Dionysus replies, "To the buzzards!" (34). Charon refuses to take Xanthias because he is a slave, so he takes an alternate route and plans to meet Dionysus at the Withering Stone.

Charon tells Dionysus to help row, and informs him that they will soon hear the songs of the Frog Swans.

Contest with Frogs

A chorus of frogs enters, and leaps around the boat, singing nonsense words like croaks. This was a song they once sung for Dionysus, or Nysean son of Zeus. Dionysus, still disguised as Heracles, mocks them. They respond that the Muses, Pan, and Apollo cherish them. Dionysus says his butt hurts and he wants them to stop singing, but they sing louder about hopping and swimming.

Dionysus finally bellows along with them in the spirit of competition. When the frogs depart, he yells that they will never beat him at the "koax" (the croaking word) and he will vanquish them.

Analysis

So begins *Frogs*, one of Aristophanes's greatest comedies and an exemplar of Old Attic Comedy. In this first scene some of the themes of the work are already present –the value of poetry and the ineffectiveness, in Aristophanes's opinion, of the current poets; the journey archetype; the jesting but competitive relationship between Xanthias and Dionysus. However, it would be a mistake to interpret the play in modern terms –i.e., character development, recognizable dramatic elements, etc. –because it is a work of ancient poetry and is thus a product of a time very different from our own. Furthermore, what playwrights intended, what audiences expected, and shared cultural and historical contemporary realities were also quite different and have caused scholars much labor as they try to identify them and translate the language for modern audiences. Part of the critical body of work, and this study guide, on *Frogs* is looking at the conventions of Greek drama and how the play may have been inspired, staged, and reviewed.

Aristophanes was a keen observer and commentator on the events of his day, which necessitates unpacking some of the references to people and events in *Frogs*. First, the play was written and is set during the Peloponnesian War between Athens and Sparta; the theme of Athens's problems and decline is present throughout the play. The battle of Arginusae occurred in 413 and although it was technically a victory for the Athenians, it came at a huge cost. Slaves were promised their freedom if they would step in a row the ships after all other manpower was exhausted, but it did not prevent Athens from losing twenty-five ships and five thousand men. The eight commanders were sentenced to death, but Athenians soon transferred their guilt onto the two men who ordered the sentences, Theramenes and Thrasybulus. In this first scene, Xanthias references the battle by bemoaning, "Blast my luck, why wasn't I in the sea battle? / Then I'd be telling *you* to go to hell!" (24).

Two other men associated with Athens's situation are mentioned throughout the play and bear a longer identification. Alcibiades was the naval leader during the war since 411, but went into voluntary exile in 407; the discussion of his recall is important in the contest between Aeschylus and Euripides at the end of the play. The other man, Cleophon, was a demagogue who persuaded the Athenians to reject Sparta's peace offering. The Chorus denigrates his actions.

Aristophanes also references works of famous tragedians and comedians, such as Euripides, Agathon (a playwright successful in his debut who recently left Athens with his lover), Xenocles (the son of the tragic poet Carcinus, whose dramatic work defeated Euripides in 415), and Morsimus (son of the tragic poet Philocles and lambasted for being a bad poet). Charon, not to mention Dionysus and Heracles, is no doubt familiar to students of Virgil's work and the overall pantheon of the Greek gods and goddesses and their accompanying body of myths and stories.

The tumultuous military situation was clearly dire, but, as scholars point out, so was the status of great tragedy. Jeffrey Henderson writes, "Aristophanes considered the situation on the tragic stage to be comparable to the military situation," as Euripides had recently died and Aeschylus had died some forty years past. Aristophanes's belief that Athens needed a poet is manifested in Dionysus's lines (in which he quotes Euripides's *Oeneus*), "I need a talented poet, / 'for some are gone, and those that lie are bad'" (27) and "But if you look for a potent poet, one who could utter / a lordly phrase, you won't find any left...potent, as in one / who can give voice to something adventuresome" (28). This desire for a poet, initially Euripides, then Aeschylus, links the two parts of the play, the journey to Hades and the contest, together.

The contest with the frogs is celebrated in literature (see "About 'Frogs'"). Questions remain about its staging; some critics suggest there were people dressed up as frogs onstage, while others believe only their voices were heard. Another suggestion is that, in order to mimic actual frogs' antiphonal croaking, one group sang "brekekekex" and the other sang "koax koax" in return. The frogs provide humor in a scene characterized by farce. The play grows more serious as it continues, but the early scenes are paragons of comedy.

The Frogs Scene II Summary and Analysis

Scene II

The boat arrives at its destination and Dionysus pays Charon. Charon departs. Xanthias meets with Dionysus again, and the latter asks about his trip around the lake. Xanthias suggests moving as to avoid the fearsome beasts, but Dionysus scoffs that Heracles was just trying to frighten him. In fact, he would welcome an encounter with a beast like that to have a story to boast about.

Xanthias cries out that he sees one, and Dionysus, panicked, orders him to get between himself and the creature. Xanthias says it is a shape-shifter, changing from a cow to a mule and a woman, and then a bitch. Dionysus says it must be Empusa (a female bogey), and Xanthias proceeds to describe her appearance.

Xanthias cries out, "Lord Heracles, we're done for!" (42) and Dionysus chides him not to use his name. When Xanthias uses "Dionysus" instead, his master is even more annoyed. Xanthias says the woman is gone, and even swears this when Dionysus asks him to.

Dionysus is shaken by this encounter, and wonders aloud why he is beset by these woes and which gods he should blame for his undoing. Suddenly the two men hear the sound of pipes, and offstage the Chorus of Initiates calls the name of "Iacchus" (the Eleusinian cult name of Dionysus). Dionysus and Xanthias decide to listen off to the side, doing nothing until they feel comfortable.

Parodos of the Chorus

The Chorus sings about Iacchus in his abode, singing with his revelers and dancing, full of "fun-loving worship" in a dance that is "pure and holy to pious Initiates" (44). They continue, singing of old men throwing off their cares and how they desire Dionysus to carry a torch and lead them to the "blooming meadowland" (45).

The Chorus Leader chants a list of all those who should not partake in their dances: those with impure attitudes, those who know nothing of these things, those uninitiated into the Bacchic rites, those who jest or enjoy jests delivered at the wrong times, those who do nothing to stop factionalism or do not act peaceably toward their fellow citizens, officials who sell out their own cities, collectors of high taxes, traitors, those who do not respect offerings made to Hecate, and politicians who do not respect the poets.

The Chorus sings of moving on now that they have breakfasted, and exalting the Savior Goddess (Athena) with their voices. The Chorus Leader calls for a song for Demeter. In this song they call for Iacchus to come with them to the goddess, for he once "found a way for us / to frolic and dance without charge" (47). They end their verses by saying they saw a pretty girl with a breast popping out of her dress.

Dionysus is excited by this and says he wants to play with her as he dances.

The Chorus suggests getting together to mock Archedemus, Cleisthenes's son, and Callias. Dionysus finally approaches and asks if they know where Pluto dwells, as they are strangers to this place.

The Chorus says he is at the door. It then commands him to go in to Demeter's "sacred circle" (49) while they will "go with the girls and the women, / to carry the sacred flame where they revel all night for the / goddess" (49).

Analysis

Before analyzing the content of the scene, it bears identifying more of the figures Aristophanes mentions in the play. Empusa is a term for a female bogey that was a part of the Eleusinian Mysteries (see Additional Content). Empusa as an individual was a demigoddess, the daughter of Hecate who seduced young men and feasted on their blood. Her name was later given to these female bogeys, which guarded roadways and ambushed travelers. Iacchus, mentioned by the Chorus of Initiates, refers to the Eleusinian cult name of Dionysus. The hymn of Diagoras refers to a lyric poem by the noted atheist, which criticized the Mysteries. Cratinus was the superlative comic poet the generation before Aristophanes. Demeter, of course, was the goddess of the earth and the mother of Persephone, married to Hades (Pluto in the play). Archedemus was one of the prosecutors of the Arginusae commanders. There is no known son of Cleisthenes, as scholar Jeffrey Henderson points out.

One of the elements of the play that may surprise modern readers is its crassness. There are slang terms for genitals, references to homosexuality, and jokes and instances pertaining to bodily functions. This was not at all uncommon for works of Greek comedy, which were known for their ease of restrictions regarding language or themes. The plays were commonly rendered in colloquial language, although they often parodied other forms of art, such as tragic poetry. During the period of Old Comedy, which began in 486 BCE and ended in 388 BCE, many of the works, such as *Frogs*, were political comedies. Other favored subjects included domestic scenes and burlesque mythological stories.

The crassness and humor seen in comedies was a reflection of the complete freedom of speech Athenians enjoyed during this period. The only thing, ironically, that Athenians could not say was anything negative about the demos' rule or anything that would harm the democracy or the state. Slander laws were not about protecting individuals; instead, they protected the state. Scholar Jeffrey Henderson notes, "if the criticism and abuse we find in Old Comedy often sees outrageous by our standards, it is because we differ from the fifth-century Athenians in our definition of outrageous, not because comic poets were held to no standards."

In Scene II the amusing and competitive relationship between Dionysus and Xanthias continues. Dionysus proves himself a boastful and bombastic figure, but one also afraid of monsters and prone to soiling himself in fear. This was no doubt hilarious to audiences in ancient Greece. Xanthias's boldness of speech is a precursor to the wisecracking slave figure ubiquitous in New Comedy.

Following Scene II is the parodos of the chorus. The term 'parodos' refers to the entrance for the chorus to either the stage or the orchestra. It also refers to the chorus's first song sung as they enter from the side. In the parodos of *Frogs*, the chorus is comprised of the Initiates, part of the Eleusinian Mysteries. They celebrate Iacchus and Demeter, and sing of those who shall not be allowed to participate in their rituals and rites. Also befitting the theme of the play, they criticize Athenians who behave badly and dishonor the state. John E. Thorburn Jr. writes, "Aristophanes shows no sympathy for people who make their living by exploiting certain situations or taking advantage of other people...[such as] those who profit from the war with Sparta, people who manipulate religion or poplar superstition for their own benefit, and professional informants."

The Frogs Scene III Summary and Analysis

Scene III

Dionysus and Xanthias are at the door of Pluto's palace. Aeacus's voice asks who is there, and when Dionysus says it is Heracles, Aeacus spews out vile curses at him. His voice fades.

Dionysus has shit himself in fear and Xanthias mocks him for being a coward. Xanthias says he was not afraid of the rants and threats, so Dionysus says that he ought to take the club and lion skin and impersonate him. Xanthias agrees and dons the disguise.

A maid comes outside, full of sweetness and charm for Heracles. Xanthias is hesitant to enter until he hears that there are dancing girls inside. He orders Dionysus to grab the luggage.

Dionysus is annoyed and asks if Xanthias really thought he, a slave, could be the son of Alcmene and Zeus. He takes back the disguise.

The Chorus enters and speaks lines about a man with sense who realizes the ship is rollicking and goes to the soft side to ride it out; this makes him like Theramenes.

A female innkeeper and her maid appear. The innkeeper calls for Plathane, who arrives with her maid. They excoriate Dionysus-as-Heracles for his past visits and greedy behavior. Xanthias enjoys this and adds his own commentary.

The innkeeper calls for her patron Cleon to come, and Plathane calls for hers, Hyperbolus, as well. Both women speak of the terrible things they want to do to Heracles, and exit.

Dionysus begs Xanthias to be Heracles again, and promises that if he asks for the disguise back he will "die a sorry death and be eradicated, / and my wife and kids" (56). Xanthias accepts this and dons the disguise again.

The Chorus warns Xanthias to be careful, and to regain his formidable demeanor. Xanthias tells them he knows Dionysus might ask for the disguise back.

Aeacus and two slaves burst out, and Aeacus orders Xanthias-as-Heracles to be bound. After a scuffle, he is subdued. Xanthias tells them to take his slave and torture him, and he will do no wrong. Aeacus asks how to torture him, and Xanthias provides a few options.

Aeacus plans to torture Dionysus in front of Xanthias, but Dionysus proclaims that he is immortal because he is a god, the son of Zeus, and Xanthias is a slave. As both claim they are gods now, Aeacus decides to torture both and see who can feel pain, which means he is a human.

Aeacus tortures both, and they utter a few noises and groans but attribute them to other causes, such as reciting a line of poetry or smelling onions. Finally, Aeacus says he cannot decide who is a god, and says that he will take them inside to Pherrephatta, who will recognize the true god. Dionysus says it is a good plan, but wishes it were thought of before the torture.

Parabasis of the Chorus

The Chorus asks the Muse to inspire joy in their song.

The Chorus Leader says it is good for the Chorus to give advice to the city. The advice includes: all citizens should be equal and any fears of being prosecuted for attacks they made under the oligarchy of 411 be erased; no one in the city should be disenfranchised; that those who participated in the sea battle of Arginusae be pardoned their misadventure; that all people embrace those who fought aboard their ships and not be too proud.

The Chorus marvels at how the city treats its citizens the same way it treats new and old coinage. Both of the coinages are unalloyed, but the city does not use the fine, new coins, but instead uses the old, low-quality ones. This is the same with the citizens, because they acknowledge the heroic and upstanding ones but treat them poorly. The Chorus cautions them to "change your ways and once again choose the good / people" (64).

Analysis

In this scene Dionysus and Xanthias continue their journey, arriving at the door to Hades and experiencing the aftermath of Heracles's own journey there in the past. There are amusing cases of assumed and mistaken identities, jesting between master and servant, and, following the scene, the parabasis of the chorus, which provides insightful commentary on the status of Athenian democracy.

As usual, some background information is helpful to understand the scene. Heracles had journeyed to Hades as one of his twelve labors; he was instructed to take Cerberus from Pluto, thus garnering the ire of Pluto and Aeacus (Aeacus explodes at Dionysus dressed as Hercules, "You're the one who rustled our dog Cerberus, / grabbed him by the throat, darted off, and got clean away, / the dog that I was in charge of!" (50). The Chorus refers to Theramines, who was a politician nicknamed "Buskin" (for a boot that fits either foot); he had helped to form and then bring about the downfall of the Four Hundred, and also put the blame on his colleagues for Arginusae. Cleon was a prominent politician of the 420s (BCE, as are subsequent dates), known for his support of ordinary citizens. Hyperbolus was his successor, and a butt of comedic poets' jokes. Hipponax was a celebrated 6th century poet.

Cleophon was a popular and influential politician after democracy was restored in 410, and he was executed in 404 on false charges brought about by anti-democratic factions. When the Chorus talks about citizenship, they are referring to refugees of the Spartan massacre at Platea in 479 receiving Athenian citizenship.

One of the notable themes of the play is identity, which is unsurprising given the fact that mistaken and switched identity was a popular element of Greek theater. It is not only amusing but can propel the plot forward, provide insight into characters' motivations, and act as a mode of conveying the poet's satiric intent. Dionysus wears the Heracles costume from the very beginning, causing the actual Heracles no end of amusement. The Greek audience would no doubt have appreciated all of the hilarity and confusion that stems from the disguise. Xanthias and Dionysus trade the costume several times as they journey into Hades, and, as Thomas K. Hubbard writes, "identity swaps function to punctuate their negotiation of the journey through its constitutive encounters."

Dionysus uses the switches of costume to bring about his desires, such as avoiding pain and procuring pleasure. Hubbard notes that he is self-serving, as his costuming is done to make his journey as easy as possible. His naiveté, cowardice, and self-interest are revealed through his readiness to wear the costume of another, or to take it off at a moment's notice when it no longer serves him. Hubbard also sees the "assuming and discarding of identity" as a "self-reflecting device, contributing to the overall effect by which the play indicates it is conscious of itself as a text and a performance."

Following Scene III is the parabasis of the chorus. A ‘parabasis’ comes when the dramatic actors leave the stage and only the chorus is there to speak to the audience. It discourses on something occasionally not directly related to the events of the play. It usually features three songs. The parabasis died out after the Old Comedy period after the chorus waned in popularity. The main point of the parabasis in *Frogs* is to discuss contemporary affairs. The Chorus asks the people of Athens to restore the rights of citizenship to those whom the oligarchic rulers disenfranchised; in particular, Cleophon is denigrated. They also excoriate Athenians for letting the wrong men do important tasks. The parabasis offers Aristophanes's most potent commentary on the state of Athens.

The Frogs Scene IV Summary and Analysis

Scene IV

Pluto's slave and Xanthias talk together. The slave marvels at how Dionysus did not beat Xanthias when he pretended to be the master, and then shares how he loves to talk about his own master behind his back. He also loves meddling, complaining, and eavesdropping.

Impressed, Xanthias asks to share kisses on the hand. He then wonders about all the noise coming from inside the palace. The slave explains a big event is starting. In the event, which is a custom, there is contest where the best professional is entitled to the Prytaneum and privileged seating next to Pluto. Aeschylus holds the Chair of Tragedy, but recently Euripides came down and starting reciting verses to the ne'er-do-wells and became very popular. The public wanted a trial to decide who is best, and Pluto agreed.

Xanthias asks why Sophocles did not bid for the chair, and the slave replies he was content to sit it out to curry favor with Aeschylus. Now, the slave explains, "poetic art will be weighed up in a balance" (68).

Xanthias inquires who the judge will be, and, as there is a "shortage of competent people" (68), the slave explains, Dionysus was chosen for his familiarity with poetry. The two men go inside.

The Chorus speaks of rivals in art, and how one artist is like a raging elephant, who has a "formidable brow frowning" and "with a roar he will hurl / utterances bolted together, tearing off timbers / with his gigantic blast" (69).

Analysis

This short scene is a transition between the first part of the play, Dionysus's journey to the underworld, and the second part of the play, Dionysus's judging of the poetic contrast between Euripides and Aeschylus. It links these otherwise seemingly unrelated plot points, and offers an amusing insight into how slaves thought and acted, at least in Aristophanes' mind. Pluto's slave revels in his criticisms of his master and his subversive behavior, boasting, "Why it's like nirvana / whenever I curse my master behind his back!" (65). Such statements would no doubt have entertained the citizens of Athens. The slave is not merely a humorous device; rather, he provides the necessary exposition for the coming contest, explaining that Euripides is challenging Aeschylus for the Chair of Tragedy and that the denizens of the underworld desire a match between the poets. The slave also informs Xanthias that his own master was chosen to be the judge, indicating how slaves seem to be privy to all of the goings-on of their masters.

The play is commonly discussed in terms of the rite of passage motif. Richard F. Moorton, Jr. explains how Dionysus traveling to the underworld embodies this. Dionysus leaves his own, profane realm and journeys into another, sacred realm; at that point, the sacred and profane switch places and his former home becomes sacred. Dionysus is a novice, untutored in the ways of Hades and thus seeks counsel from Heracles, a wiser figure as he had already traveled there. Dionysus experiences his mock, comic, and symbolic death, which is enacted, ritual-like, through his rowing himself across the Styx. He crosses through this neutral zone between realms and encounters the frogs, which belong to neither zone. Moorton comments that the frogs are "both witnesses of Dionysus's rite of passage and participants in it: by virtue of their rhythmical singing they are supposedly facilitators, actually comic obstructers, of his rowing."

Once in Hades, before he gets to Pluto's door, Dionysus must survive a monster –the Empusa –resist the temptation to revel with the Initiates. Having completed those tasks, he experiences an identity crisis of sorts as he confronts the various individuals who answer Pluto's door. He learns that he will not be able to simply kidnap Euripides or perform some action of "larcenous chicanery", as Moorton calls it, but instead has a different role to embody. This is the role of judge, of arbiter. He is now in Hades as a friend of Pluto, and has been given this task in order to help stabilize the realm, which is suffering due to the rivalry between poets. Dionysus accepts his role and in the process of the contest, learns more about the nature of tragedy and what kind of tragic poet can help Athens in her hour of need. It is no longer Euripides, whom he actually came down to procure, but Aeschylus instead.

The entire point of a rite of passage journey is regeneration, and while that happens for Dionysus, who returns to the world above, it is suggested that it happens for Athens as a whole, now that Aeschylus is returning to guide and counsel the city-state back to its preeminence and power.

Finally, many critics have also wondered about the atypical structure of the play in terms of comedy and tragedy, for in *Frogs* the major agony comes after the parabasis, and the funny scenes come before. However, Thomas K. Hubbard explains, "Aristophanes may have structured the play as he did precisely to make a point about the relation of the comic and the serious...and the necessity of approaching the serious through the comic." In that case, Aristophanes can be lauded even more for his “meta” approach to his plays –understanding that they are not simply a series of events and obvious morals, but because they can, within the structure of the play itself, offer profound insight into the way the world does, and should, work.

The Frogs Contests Summary and Analysis

Contest: Preliminaries

Three chairs are onstage. Pluto sits in the center chair, Dionysus on his left and Aeschylus on his right. Euripides touches Aeschylus's chair and says he will not let go because he is better than the other poet. Euripides continues, calling him a "creator of savages, a boorish loudmouth, / with an unbridled, unruly, ungated mouth" (70). Outraged, Aeschylus says Euripides is a "babble collector, / you creator of beggars, you stitcher of old rags" (70).

Dionysus mediates between them, giving them both warnings. Aeschylus sniffs that this is not a contest of equal terms because "my poetry hasn't died with me, / while his is as dead as he is" (72).

Contest: Opening Rituals

Dionysus proclaims that he will judge this contest with integrity, and calls for the Chorus to sing to the Muses. Each poet prays -- Aeschylus to Demeter and Euripides to Sky, Smarts, and Pivot of Tongue.

Contest: General Issues

The Chorus says it is ready to hear the wild tongues of the poets, with their sharp arguments and bold spirits. Euripides plans to expose his rival as "the charlatan and quack he was" (74). He mocks Aeschylus's having silent characters, rattling off four suites of choral lyric in a row, and his obnoxious use of big words. He also lampoons his "huge craggy utterances" (75) and his writing about a rooster in a tragedy.

Aeschylus asks what Euripides wrote about, and the latter explains that when he inherited the pompous, inflated art from Aeschylus, he put it on a diet. He also never wrote the first thing that just popped into his head. He never left characters idle, and taught the spectators how to talk. His poetry is rooted in the everyday, and he "never distracted their mind with bombastic bluster" (77). He also claims to teach people how to think because his art is rational and critical; thus, people know how to order their affairs because of him.

The Chorus quotes a line of Aeschylus' at him, and warns him not to be too angry in return.

Aeschylus replies that he is enraged and annoyed to even have to debate Euripides, but he proceeds to ask him what qualities a poet should be admired for. When Euripides responds, "skill and good counsel" because they make people better, Aeschylus tells him that he has actually ruined people. He believes his own work is an achievement on par with the noble poets of the past. He boasts that he has never created a whorish woman. It is his belief that a poet "has a special duty to conceal / what's wicked / not stage it or teach it " (82).

Euripides criticizes Aeschylus's high language, but the latter replies that "great thoughts / and ideas force us to produce expressions that are equal to them" (82). He scoffs at Euripides's poetry and its making people more prone to chitchat, and women behaving poorly. His work is full of "assistant secretaries / and clownish monkeys of politicians / forever lying to the people" (84).

Dionysus laughs at the memory of a crass work of Euripides, having been mocking, teasing, and riling up the two poets throughout their war of words.

Contest: Prologues

The Chorus sings of this great war, and prepares itself for more parries and thrusts. It exalts the spectators, who are clever enough to understand what is going on.

Euripides begins by examining one of Aeschylus's prologues –a line from the *Oresteia*. He has numerous criticisms of the lines, even though they are very short. In the lines of "Underworld Hermes, who watch over the paternal domain, / be now, I pray, my ally and my savior, / for I've come back to this land and now return" (85), Euripides finds mistakes in Hermes's role as well as the repetition of ideas. Aeschylus believes his wording is excellent.

Euripides recites some of his own lines about Oedipus, which Aeschylus picks apart as well.

Aeschylus says he can take the simple phrase "oil bottle" and tack it on to any of Euripides's prologues, which he does so to the great amusement of Dionysus; one example is Euripides reciting "Once Oeneus from his land reaped a bounteous harvest, / and while sacrificing his first fruits –" (92) and Aeschylus throwing in "lost his oil bottle" (92) at the end. Finally, Dionysus asks the attention to be turned to lyrics. Euripides smugly says Aeschylus has nothing new here.

Contest: Lyrics

Euripides begins by saying all of Aeschylus's lyrics have the same pattern; he gives a few examples from the *Myrmidons* and *Ghost Riders*. He gives a few more, and Dionysus says he feels sore from all these strikes levied. He asks Aeschylus where he collected these "rope-winders' songs" (94). Aeschylus replies that they were from a reputable source for a good reason, unlike Euripides, who borrows willy-nilly from everywhere.

The Muse of Euripides enters. Both poets continue to criticize each other's lyrics, with Aeschylus ending by looking at the meter of Euripides's arias.

Contest: Weighing of the Verses

Dionysus calls for the verses to stop –it is time to weigh them. He compares it selling cheese, but has the poets come to the scales anyway. Each speaks a line, and Aeschylus's goes lower, as he spoke of the river and haunts. The second time they speak, and Aeschylus's still goes lower, as he spoke of Death. Euripides, who evoked Persuasion, is annoyed.

In the final weighing, Aeschylus is victorious again with his lines of "Chariot upon chariot, and corpse upon corpse" (99). Aeschylus laughs that Euripides could put his whole family and books in, and he would still lose.

Contest: Politics

Dionysus still finds it difficult to choose which poet he prefers. Pluto tells him he may take the one he chooses back with him, so he asks the two poets how they feel about Alcibiades. Euripides says he abhors the citizen who is slow to help his country but harms her instead. Aeschylus contributes a pithy statement about how a city should not rear a lion cub, but if it does, it must cater to it.

Dionysus then asks how they would save the city. Euripides laughingly suggests spraying vinegar in the eyes of their enemies, then adds that he suggests letting other people who currently are not in charge try their hand at ruling. Aeschylus, for his part, says that the bad people and good people are not doing much for their city.

Contest: Verdict

Dionysus proclaims that he is choosing Aeschylus. Euripides is furious, and curses Dionysus. Dionysus uses his own lines back at him, and Euripides exits.

Bon Voyage to Aeschylus

Pluto offers a banquet to Dionysus and Aeschylus before the latter sets sail. The Chorus praises the poet, a man of intelligence, clear sight, and good sense who is now going back to his people.

Pluto says goodbye to Aeschylus and encourages him to save the city with his sage advice and educate the witless. He lists a few men and encourages Aeschylus to tell them to hurry down to him.

Aeschylus instructs Pluto to hand his chair over to Socrates to look after it, "for I rank him / second to me in the art" (106). He warns him not to let Euripides anywhere near the chair.

The Chorus sings for Aeschylus to have a good voyage above to the sunlight that that "we may have an end of great griefs / and painful encounters in arms" (107).

Analysis

Dionysus' journey to the underworld ends with him bringing back a poet to help Athens, but interestingly enough, it is not the poet he intended. This last section of contests helps Dionysus mature and come to a better understanding of what his city-state needs, and also advances several significant critiques of tragedy and the poet's role in society and politics. Aristophanes' views on what kind of poetry would best serve Athens could not be clearer by the end of *Frogs*.

Euripides and Aeschylus are two names no doubt familiar to most students of history and/or literature. Euripides was known for his 92 plays (only 19 are extant), which included *The Trojan Women*, *The Bacchae*, and *Medea*. His characters were often passionate and flawed, and were usually members of the common folk. Aeschylus was a more traditional poet, whose 80+ plays (7 are extant) include the *Oresteia* trilogy and *Prometheus Bound*. He was known for his moral themes and advice for his audience to conduct themselves in an upright fashion befitting citizens of the great Athenian demos.

Aristophanes was quite familiar with the work of both of these poets, and the critiques hurled from one to the other reflect generally established truisms regarding their respective work. Euripides claims Aeschylus is a "creator of savages, a boorish loudmouth" (70) who was prone to "come out with a dozen words as big as an ox" (74) and "huge craggy utterances / that weren't easy to decipher" (75). He says he put Aeschylus's weight prose on a diet and did not "write whatever humbug entered my head" (76). He believes that because he wrote about everyday scenes and real people that he was the better poet; there is no reason to distract the readers with "bombastic bluster" (77). He encouraged people to think critically and rationally, he also claims. Aeschylus places himself within the tradition of noble poets, believing his work to be grander and moral. His works, full of great thoughts and ideas, inspire the audience, while Euripides writes of wanton women and is beloved by quacks and the simpleminded.

Dionysus cannot decide between the two of them, and thus has the poets weigh their verses. As Aeschylus recites deeper and more profound verse, he bests Euripides. The final point of debate is about Alcibiades, and Aeschylus's views win the day. As the Chorus extols, he is a "man who has / keen intelligence" and "eminent good sense" (105) and who will now return to Athens to help guide the floundering city. His poetry will teach, as it has done, people to be courageous in battle, and loyal more generally.

Aristophanes' choice reflects, of course, his views on what Athens needs. Scholar James Redfield writes, "The conflict between Aeschylus and Euripides is a poetic expression of the conflict between old and new politics, and the victory of Aeschylus is a rejection of the new life-style, a return to the old moral center." There is not a current need for Euripides's cleverness or originality, or his neutrality in politics as well as the art of tragedy. Because for Euripides "there is no order either in community or in the world", he is not a good choice to *restore* the order that Aristophanes and Athens crave.

The Frogs The Eleusinian Mysteries

The Eleusinian Mysteries are one of the most compelling and fascinating cultural artifacts of ancient Greece. Their origins are found in the Homeric *Hymn to Demeter*. In this Homeric, Demeter, goddess of the earth, travels to Eleusis to find her daughter Persephone, who was abducted by Hades, the god of the underworld. While Demeter is gone, the earth languishes and the gods become worried. Zeus intervenes; however, Hades has Persephone eat a pomegranate, which connects her to Hades for a third of every year. Also in her journey, Demeter befriends the royal family of Eleusis and agrees to bring up the queen's son. She plans to make the boy eternally young, but when the boy's mother finds out she reveals herself as the goddess and demands a temple be built for her. Overall, the themes of the Mysteries revolve around honoring Demeter and hoping for life after death.

When Eleusis was incorporated into Athens, that city took charge of the festival to honor Demeter, although it retained its local flavor. A holy truce was called for fifty-five days for all of the Greek city-states.

The Mysteries start with the Initiates' march from Athens to Eleusis. There, at the Hall of Initiation (the Telesterion), the rites were performed. It is unknown precisely what happened in these rites, although they did begin with purification rites, called the Lesser Mysteries and held at Agrai outside of Athens in February-March. The Greater Mysteries were held in September-October and included bathing in the sea, fasting for three days, and another, more complicated and ambiguous rite. Sacred objects, called the Hiera, were used, stored in a temple near the Acropolis in Athens before the celebration and carried along with the procession. Shouts of "Iacchus", identified as Dionysus, the avatar of excitement and energy, were shouted; some other versions of the myths said Iacchus was the son of Demeter or Persephone. The rituals within the Telesterion were secret, only revealed to the Initiates. It is said that the priestesses revealed the vision of the holy night and/or revealed the seeds in a stalk of grain. The fasting was also broken when the Initiates drank a potion that symbolized Demeter's refusal to imbibe red wine. On the last day (scholars estimate that there were nine) the procession returned to Athens, carrying to sacred objects.

During the Hellenistic age, the Mysteries grew even more popular. They were run by the state and aristocratic families officiated. Mystery cults were well known, and it required very little (to be without blood guilt and to understand Greek) to be an Initiate. Thousands of people participated. Men, women, and slaves were allowed to participate.

The Mysteries ended when the Roman Emperor Theodosius closed the sanctuary in 392 CE. Christianity later came to the region, and these "pagan" rites could no longer be celebrated.

The Frogs Links

The Frogs

http://classics.mit.edu/Aristophanes/frogs.html

An e-text of the play.

The Frogs

http://www.theatrehistory.com/ancient/bates029.html

A short history of the play, as well as related links, at TheatreHistory.com.

Aristophanes' Frogs Study Guide

https://www.ucl.ac.uk/classics/classical-play/archive/2009Frogs-studyinfo

A short essay, study questions, and bibliography from University College London.

The Frogs Essay Questions

1. **What is the structure of the play's plot?**

   The play has two major parts. The first is the archetypal heroic journey, in which Dionysus leaves the upper world and ventures down into Hades. He is on a quest to retrieve the poet Euripides, who will return to earth and help Athens with his wise counsel. Dionysus encounters several obstacles and monsters, but makes it to his destination. In the second part, the two poets Euripides and Aeschylus engage in a series of contests in which they critique each other's verse to determine who is the best tragic poet. This fast-paced, quick-witted set of contests is judged by Dionysus, who, through this arbitration, reaches the culmination of his journey as he grows wiser and more discerning. While some critics believe the structure to be off-putting and disunified, others believe the two parts are yoked by Dionysus and his literal and emotional journey.

2. **What are the canonical messages and themes of the play?**

   In this significant work, Aristophanes deals with a number of overarching themes. He delves into the problems Athens faces, identifying some of the reasons for its decline. With that, he also explores the decline of the art form of tragedy. He offers an argument for the relevance and significance of poetry, and shares his beliefs as to what great poetry can teach the audience. In this particular theme he asserts that traditional values and morality, as exemplified by the poet Aeschylus, are necessary to buffet the distressed city-state. He also looks at the relationships between master and slave, the heroic journey, identity and disguise, ambition, and pride.

3. **What are some of the problems that Athens faces at the time of the play, according to Aristophanes?**

   The decline of Athens is one of the most prominent themes in the text. Aristophanes provides plenty of reasons for why this occurs, such as: bad military commanders, debauched and wanton poetry, politicians like Theramenes who take the easy way out when things get tough, problems for citizens such as disenfranchisement and punishment, Athens's propensity to elevate lesser citizens to positions of power rather than support those who are worthy, weakness in battle, and more. He hopes that the words of Aeschylus can counter the deleterious effects all of these have had on Athens, and that the city can once more be glorious and powerful.

4. **What insights can the reader gain from Xanthias' status and behavior in the play?**

Xanthias is not your average slave -- he is feisty, opinionated, and feels confident in talking back to his master. He serves several important functions in the text. First, he is Dionysus's able-bodied adjutant on the god's trip to the underworld; Xanthias carries his baggage and helps him when threatened by the monster Empusa. He also wears the Heracles costume when Dionysus is needs him to. Second, his character provides insights into the master-servant relationship and how slaves were treated in ancient Greece. Third, he provides comic relief. Because he speaks his mind and tells Dionysus exactly what he thinks of him, he is funny and provocative. His feelings toward Dionysus often mirror the audience's, and he voices such shared feelings and reactions. While he is not significant at all in the second part of the play, he is an indispensable component of the first.

5. **How would the play have been staged in traditional Greek theater?**

There were several mainstays of the production of an ancient Greek Old Comedy. The actors would wear masks, most generic but occasionally, if the person was notable, a portrait mask. The clothing was suited to their identities in the play, but in comedies, a few things were added to heighten the humor -a big stomach and a rump, and the phallos, a large penis. It was usually made of leather and was often dangling, sometimes erect if the scene called for it. All the female roles were played by men, who would wear bodysuits depicting female genitalia. Most of the comedies only had three actors, who switched roles. The chorus consisted of twenty-four men, who also wore masks and costumes. They sang with the accompaniment of an aulos, a wind instrument. The chorus also danced if required by the text. The comedy was played through without intermission and was about two hours long.

6. **What is the historical background to the original staging of the play?**

The two occasions for which comedies were produced were two festivals honoring Dionysus -the Greater Dionysia, in late March or early April, and the Lenaea, late January or early February. The productions in these festivals were competitions where the great poets would show their new work and compete for the top prize. The Greater Dionysia was held in the Theater of Dionysus on the slope of the Acropolis; both citizens and foreigners attended. The Lenaea was only for Athenians, and was held at the same Theater beginning in the 4th century BCE. Comedy, tragedy, and satyr-drama were performed. The comedies were the least restricted by convention or norm. One of the most important offices in the demos, the choregus, was the sponsor of the chorus. They paid for everything that went into the play, and were thus vehicles for such men to display their wealth. The stipends for the poet and the actors and prizes were paid for by the demos. A poet submitted his draft for the play six months in advance, but revisions occurred frequently. The poet acted as music master, choreographer, and director.

7. **How do the figure and acts of Alcibiades influence the play?**

Alcibiades was such a polarizing figure around the time *Frogs* was written that Aristophanes could not help referring to him both obliquely and explicitly. In the final contest between Euripides and Aeschylus, the topic turns to politics, and Dionysus asks, "So, for starters, which of you has an opinion about / Alcibiades? The city's in travail about him" (101). Alcibiades was an aristocratic military commander who was in charge of the Sicilian Expedition but fled to Sparta to avoid being prosecuted for disrespecting the Eleusinian Mysteries. In 411 he left the Spartans and returned to Athens, where he was elected commander by the Fleet. In 407 he became Supreme Commander but was dismissed after a major defeat. In 404 he was assassinated. At the time of the play, his recall from Athens was continually discussed and debated by the Athenians. Euripides criticizes him, but Aeschylus seems to appreciate his brilliance, and believes that if Athens allowed him, who was like a lion cub, to exist at all, it should "cater to its ways" (101).

8. **What is parabasis, and what does it accomplish in the play?**

A parabasis in a Greek comedy is when the chorus comes onstage, removes their masks, and talks to the audience about a weighty topic, usually not related to the action of the play. The Chorus Leader speaks, and the Chorus sings. In the parabasis of *Frogs*, the information given is all about the trials and travails of Athens. While not directly related to the action, it is actually a very helpful accounting of the reasons *why* Dionysus needs to go down to Hades and find a poet, and why he ends up choosing Aeschylus. The Chorus speaks of making citizens equal and not disenfranchising them, and brings up the case of those pardoned for their role in the sea battle. At the end of the parabasis, the Chorus Leader bemoans the fact that Athens does not treat its best citizens well, and instead "we choose... / bad people with bad ancestors, / the latest arrivals" (65). The parabasis thus gives the audience (and readers) a look at the historical context of the play and adds weight to its content.

9. **What are the critiques and criticisms of Euripides's and Aeschylus's lyrics and prologues?**

Two of the contests deal with the actual parts of the tragedies written by Euripides and Aeschylus -the lyrics and the prologues. A prologue is a monologue or a dialogue preceding the entrance of the chorus, where the topic of tragedy is presented to the audience. Euripides believes that Aeschylus is too obscure in his plots, and makes too many errors, such as saying the same thing twice. Aeschylus's critique is more amusing, showing how all of Euripides's prologue lines are predictable and could all end with the same phrase containing "oil bottle". As for lyrics, Euripides says he can "trim all his lyrics down to a single pattern" (93), prompting Dionysus to ask, "Where did / you collect these rope-winders' songs?"

(94). Aeschylus says that Euripides's lyrics are too wanton, that his arias are too suggestive. These critiques might seem a bit obscure to modern audiences, but they are nonetheless incisive and amusing.

10. **How does *Frogs* utilize specific comedic devices to convey its messages?**

Frogs is a masterful example of Old Attic Comedy. It relies on a few devices to achieve its comedic effect. First, it is crass, using humor that revolves around excrement, flatulence, and sex. Second, it uses amusing costumes and cases of mistaken identity, as when Dionysus, dressed as Heracles, is both yelled at and propositioned, and when Xanthias and Dionysus trade the costume and are tortured. Third, it reveals the two sides of Dionysus, making the audience revel in his cowardly nature while appreciating his energy and dynamic personality. Fourth, the contest between the poets uses keen, intellectual humor in the jabs and critiques levied by each. Here the audience recognizes the humor, but it is a far different humor than the one that derives from hearing that Dionysus crapped his pants in fear of the Empusa.

The Frogs Quizzes

1. **What year was Frogs written?**
    A. 406 BCE
    B. 420 BCE
    C. 405 CE
    D. 405 BCE

2. **The play is an example of**
    A. New Comedy
    B. Reformed Comedy
    C. Old Comedy
    D. Middle Comedy

3. **The play was written amidst**
    A. the Trojan War
    B. the Great War
    C. the Peleponnesian Wars
    D. the Punic Wars

4. **In its time the play was**
    A. generally ignored
    B. well-received
    C. tolerated but not popular
    D. reviled

5. **Frogs premiered at a festival honoring**
    A. Aphrodite
    B. Demeter
    C. Athena
    D. Dionysus

6. **In ancient Greek comedies,**
    A. no slang was tolerated
    B. conventions were relaxed
    C. conventions were upheld
    D. the actors did not wear masks or costumes

7. **Aristophanes was from**
    A. Argos
    B. Athens
    C. Corinth
    D. Carthage

8. **The political system in Athens was a/an**
   A. oligarchy
   B. anarchy
   C. dictatorship
   D. democracy

9. **One of the main themes of the work is**
   A. Athens's decline
   B. the power of romantic love
   C. the rise of Christianity
   D. friendship

10. **Comedies were**
   A. often crass and controversial
   B. less popular than tragedies
   C. devoid of political commentary
   D. limited by free speech laws

11. **Who is the protagonist of the play?**
   A. Dionysus
   B. Xanthias
   C. Pluto
   D. Heracles

12. **Dionysus is dressed as**
   A. Heracles
   B. Pluto
   C. Xanthias
   D. Zeus

13. **What does Xanthias ride?**
   A. An ox
   B. A donkey
   C. A horse
   D. Nothing

14. **When Heracles sees Dionysus's costume, he**
   A. pretends he doesn't notice it
   B. criticizes its veracity
   C. bursts out laughing
   D. punches him

15. **Dionysus compares his longing for Euripides with a longing for**
   A. minestrone
   B. grapes
   C. wine
   D. meat

16. **Why does Dionysus want to get Euripides from Hades?**
    A. His lover wants him back
    B. He has a score to settle with him
    C. He has to talk to him about his fate
    D. He needs a talented poet

17. **Heracles suggests all of the following playwrights to Dionysus except**
    A. Agathon
    B. Sophocles
    C. Aeschylus
    D. Iophon

18. **Dionysus says the poet he wants must be**
    A. reserved
    B. potent
    C. witty
    D. sensitive

19. **What does Dionysus want from Heracles?**
    A. Advice about the journey to Hades
    B. Money
    C. To attain his blessing
    D. Insight into Euripides's character

20. **Heracles suggests all the following modes of suicide except**
    A. jumping off a tower
    B. hanging
    C. hemlock
    D. drowning

21. **How much does the fare to Hades cost?**
    A. Four obols
    B. Two obols
    C. Six obols
    D. Ten obols

22. **Heracles's description of Hades includes all of the following except**
    A. the damned
    B. a Chorus of Initiates
    C. a river of shit
    D. Cerberus

23. **Who does Dionysus initially try to get to carry their bags to Hades?**
    A. A corpse
    B. Cerberus
    C. Heracles
    D. The Chorus of Initiates

24. **Who is Charon?**

A. Pluto's slave
B. The ferryman on the river Styx
C. The innkeeper in Hades
D. The corpse

25. **Xanthias cannot ride in the boat because**

A. he is too fat
B. Dionysus is tired of him
C. Charon does not like him
D. he is a slave

Quiz 1 Answer Key

1. **(D)** 405 BCE
2. **(C)** Old Comedy
3. **(C)** the Peleponnesian Wars
4. **(B)** well-received
5. **(D)** Dionysus
6. **(B)** conventions were relaxed
7. **(B)** Athens
8. **(D)** democracy
9. **(A)** Athens's decline
10. **(A)** often crass and controversial
11. **(A)** Dionysus
12. **(A)** Heracles
13. **(B)** A donkey
14. **(C)** bursts out laughing
15. **(A)** minestrone
16. **(D)** He needs a talented poet
17. **(C)** Aeschylus
18. **(B)** potent
19. **(A)** Advice about the journey to Hades
20. **(D)** drowning
21. **(B)** Two obols
22. **(D)** Cerberus
23. **(A)** A corpse
24. **(B)** The ferryman on the river Styx
25. **(D)** he is a slave

The Frogs Quizzes

1. **The frogs are found**
    A. at Heracles's house
    B. at Pluto's palace
    C. in Hades
    D. on the way to Hades

2. **How does Dionysus feel about the frogs?**
    A. He tries to grab them and make them stop
    B. He is annoyed by them
    C. He thinks they are lovely
    D. He ignores them

3. **The frogs say all of the following love them except**
    A. Pan
    B. Apollo
    C. the Muses
    D. Zeus

4. **One of Dionysus's flaws is**
    A. pride
    B. apathy
    C. lack of intelligence
    D. rage

5. **Xanthias can be described as**
    A. clever
    B. humble
    C. meek
    D. venegful

6. **Empusa is a**
    A. monster
    B. place
    C. animal
    D. goddess

7. **What happens to Dionysus when he sees Empusa?**
    A. He cries
    B. He runs away
    C. He screams in fear
    D. He craps his pants

8. **Iacchus is another name for**
   A. Persephone
   B. Pluto
   C. Demeter
   D. Dionysus

9. **The Eleusinian Mysteries are**
   A. gods and goddesses
   B. rites
   C. books
   D. poems

10. **The Eleusinian Mysteries honor**
   A. Hera
   B. Demeter
   C. Athena
   D. Aphrodite

11. **The parodos is sung by**
   A. Aeschylus
   B. the Chorus
   C. Dionysus
   D. Pluto

12. **All of the following are not allowed in the Mysteries except**
   A. those with unclean attitudes
   B. those unfamiliar with the rites
   C. proponents of factionalism
   D. those who are too old

13. **Demeter is the goddess of**
   A. hunting
   B. harvests
   C. love
   D. the hearth

14. **What do the Initiates want Dionysus to do?**
   A. Go on their procession
   B. Build a temple
   C. Sing a song
   D. Talk to the frogs

15. **Who is Archedemus?**
   A. A demagogue
   B. A dictator
   C. A Spartan military commander
   D. A prosecutor of the commanders at Arginusae

16. **Who is the first person to speak to the travelers in Hades?**
A. Aeacus
B. A slave
C. Plathane
D. Pluto

17. **Aeacus hates**
A. Heracles
B. Pluto
C. Xanthias
D. Dionysus

18. **In response to Aeacus's threats,**
A. Dionysus gives Xanthias the costume
B. Dionysus challenges him to a fight
C. Dionysus leaves
D. Dionysus craps himself

19. **Dionysus asks for the costume back because of**
A. feeling cold
B. Xanthias's behavior
C. dancing girls
D. the Chorus of Initiates

20. **How does Plathane feel about Heracles?**
A. She does not know who he is
B. She is confused by him
C. She loves him
D. She hates him

21. **Cleon was a champion of**
A. the common man
B. the rich
C. the military
D. slaves

22. **Xanthias calls Dionysus a**
A. tyrant
B. beast
C. hypocrite
D. coward

23. **Frogs is known for its**
A. nonsensicality
B. wit
C. romance
D. elegance

24. **Heracles is the son of**

A. Alcemene
B. Andromeda
C. Dido
D. Arachne

25. **How does Aeacus try to find out who is a god?**

A. Offering money
B. Asking politely
C. Torture
D. Using women

Quiz 2 Answer Key

1. **(D)** on the way to Hades
2. **(B)** He is annoyed by them
3. **(D)** Zeus
4. **(A)** pride
5. **(A)** clever
6. **(A)** monster
7. **(D)** He craps his pants
8. **(D)** Dionysus
9. **(B)** rites
10. **(B)** Demeter
11. **(B)** the Chorus
12. **(D)** those who are too old
13. **(B)** harvests
14. **(A)** Go on their procession
15. **(D)** A prosecutor of the commanders at Arginusae
16. **(A)** Aeacus
17. **(A)** Heracles
18. **(A)** Dionysus gives Xanthias the costume
19. **(C)** dancing girls
20. **(D)** She hates him
21. **(A)** the common man
22. **(D)** coward
23. **(B)** wit
24. **(A)** Alcemene
25. **(C)** Torture

The Frogs Quizzes

1. **What happens in the torture?**
   A. The men don't feel it and don't admit it
   B. The men feel it and admit it
   C. The men feel it but don't admit it
   D. The men don't feel it and admit it

2. **Hipponax was a**
   A. philosopher
   B. poet
   C. politician
   D. god

3. **Cleophon was a**
   A. philosopher
   B. military commander
   C. politician
   D. poet

4. **The parabasis concerns**
   A. romance
   B. the Trojan War
   C. politics
   D. the doings of the gods

5. **In the parabasis the Chorus wants all of the following except**
   A. those who were in Arginusae should be pardoned
   B. the democracy should be eradicated
   C. all citizens should be equal
   D. no one should be disenfranchised

6. **Arginusae was**
   A. a city
   B. a temple
   C. a battle
   D. a poet

7. **The Chorus compares bad and good men to**
   A. gods
   B. vases
   C. coins
   D. wine

8. **Those who the Chorus scorns include all of the following except**
   A. redheads
   B. poor men
   C. those with bad ancestors
   D. aliens

9. **Those whom the Chorus views as good men are all of the following except**
   A. the well-behaved
   B. wrestlers and artists
   C. the rich
   D. the well-born

10. **Pluto's slave said it was nirvana to**
   A. sing a song
   B. have sex
   C. curse his master
   D. look upon Demeter

11. **The big event down in Hades that Pluto's slave tells Xanthias about is**
   A. a party to honor Dionysus
   B. the Eleusinian Mysteries
   C. a fight between Pluto and the poets
   D. a debate between Aeschylus and Euripides

12. **Aeschylus holds the Chair of**
   A. Comedy
   B. Tragedy
   C. Philosophy
   D. Poetry

13. **Who does Xanthias ask about in terms of seeking the Chair?**
   A. Sophocles
   B. Socrates
   C. Aristophanes
   D. Plato

14. **Who is the judge of the poetic contest?**
   A. Demeter
   B. Dionysus
   C. Heracles
   D. Pluto

15. **Who says that poets shouldn't squabble?**
   A. Pluto
   B. Xanthias
   C. Dionysus
   D. Euripides

16. **Aeschylus says the contest isn't fair because**
A. his poetry hasn't died with him
B. his poetry is less famous
C. he is older
D. he is a better poet

17. **Who does Aeschylus pray to?**
A. Aphrodite
B. Artemis
C. Athena
D. Demeter

18. **Who does Euripides pray to?**
A. No one
B. Sky and Smarts
C. Demeter
D. Pluto

19. **Euripides accuses Aeschylus of all of the following except**
A. his chorus rattles off too many lines
B. big words and complicated sentences
C. writing about a rooster
D. being shallow

20. **What did Euripides say he did to poetry after Aeschylus?**
A. Put it on a shelf
B. Inflated it
C. Chastized it
D. Put it on a diet

21. **Euripides says he taught spectators to**
A. how to read poetry
B. how to fight
C. how to talk
D. how to love

22. **Euripides says his own work**
A. is traditional
B. is wanton
C. is about everyday things
D. is bombastic

23. **Aeschylus's work can best be described as**
A. controversial
B. modern
C. traditional
D. witty

24. **Euripides says his work makes people**

A. irrational
B. lazy
C. philosophical
D. rational

25. **What does Euripides think a poet should be admired for?**

A. Keen wit
B. Bombastic prose
C. Skill and good counsel
D. Morals

Quiz 3 Answer Key

1. **(C)** The men feel it but don't admit it
2. **(B)** poet
3. **(C)** politician
4. **(C)** politics
5. **(B)** the democracy should be eradicated
6. **(C)** a battle
7. **(C)** coins
8. **(B)** poor men
9. **(C)** the rich
10. **(C)** curse his master
11. **(D)** a debate between Aeschylus and Euripides
12. **(B)** Tragedy
13. **(A)** Sophocles
14. **(B)** Dionysus
15. **(C)** Dionysus
16. **(A)** his poetry hasn't died with him
17. **(D)** Demeter
18. **(B)** Sky and Smarts
19. **(D)** being shallow
20. **(D)** Put it on a diet
21. **(C)** how to talk
22. **(C)** is about everyday things
23. **(C)** traditional
24. **(D)** rational
25. **(C)** Skill and good counsel

The Frogs Quizzes

1. **What did Aeschylus's Persians teach people to do?**
   A. Be formidable in battle
   B. Pursue romantic love
   C. Worship the gods more
   D. Enjoy everyday life

2. **The "noble poets" that Aeschylus mentions include all of the following except**
   A. Sophocles
   B. Musaeus
   C. Orpheus
   D. Homer

3. **Aeschylus deplores the _________ Euripides created.**
   A. bold slaves
   B. bloodthirsty warriors
   C. craven politicians
   D. lustful women

4. **Euripides scorns that _________ had nothing to do with Aeschylus.**
   A. Athena
   B. Aphrodite
   C. Dido
   D. Hera

5. **According to Aeschylus a poet has a duty to**
   A. reveal the truth
   B. reveal wicked things
   C. conceal the truth
   D. conceal wicked things

6. **Aeschylus claims Euripides taught people to cultivate**
   A. laziness
   B. chitchat and gab
   C. crassness
   D. rationality

7. **The first prologue of Aeschylus discussed is**
   A. the Persians
   B. the Oresteia
   C. Myrmidons
   D. Seven Against Thebes

8. **An objection of Euripides to Aeschylus's prologue is**
   A. he is boring
   B. he uses big words
   C. he is wanton
   D. he says the same thing twice

9. **Euripides's recited prologue is about**
   A. Orestes
   B. Oedipus
   C. Odysseus
   D. Agamemnon

10. **Aeschylus demonstrates that all of Euripides's prologues can use the**
    A. ship mast
    B. whip
    C. oil bottle
    D. wine flask

11. **Euripides's attitude in the contest is**
    A. pleasant
    B. passive
    C. muted
    D. irreverent

12. **According to Euripides, Aeschylus's lyrics**
    A. all have the same pattern
    B. are dull and stentorian
    C. are miseading
    D. are wanton and lustful

13. **Aeschylus compares Euripides's lyrics to the work of a/an**
    A. warrior
    B. athlete
    C. courtesan
    D. god

14. **After the contest, what is the final way to judge the works?**
    A. Read them
    B. Perform them
    C. Ask the other gods
    D. Weigh them

15. **Aeschylus wins the first weighing with a line about**
    A. the river and haunts
    B. death
    C. the ship Argo
    D. a corpse

16. **Aeschylus wins the second weighing with a line about**

A. a corpse
B. death
C. the river
D. Persuasion

17. **Aeschylus wins the last weighing with a line about**

A. the river Styx
B. iron
C. corpses and chariots
D. drinking wine

18. **The last question for the poets concerns**

A. Alcibiades
B. Cleon
C. Cleisthenes
D. Pericles

19. **Aeschylys compares Alcibiaes to a/an**

A. wolf
B. monster
C. panther
D. lion cub

20. **Dionysus admires Euripides for his**

A. morality
B. cleverness
C. heavy prose
D. lurid prose

21. **How does Euripides react to the verdict?**

A. He is confused
B. He is placid
C. He is pleased
D. He is enraged

22. **Before he returns to earth, Pluto offers what to Aeschylus?**

A. A meal
B. A fur coat
C. Money
D. A handshake

23. **The Chorus condemns the "stylish" practice of sitting around with**

A. Pluto
B. Sophocles
C. Socrates
D. Plato

24. **The Chorus praises Aeschylus's**

A. wildness
B. wit
C. cleverness
D. good sense

25. **Who does Aeschylus say can hold his chair while he returns to Athens?**

A. Euripides
B. Sophocles
C. Iophon
D. Socrates

Quiz 4 Answer Key

1. **(A)** Be formidable in battle
2. **(A)** Sophocles
3. **(D)** lustful women
4. **(B)** Aphrodite
5. **(D)** conceal wicked things
6. **(B)** chitchat and gab
7. **(B)** the Oresteia
8. **(D)** he says the same thing twice
9. **(B)** Oedipus
10. **(C)** oil bottle
11. **(D)** irreverent
12. **(A)** all have the same pattern
13. **(C)** courtesan
14. **(D)** Weigh them
15. **(A)** the river and haunts
16. **(B)** death
17. **(C)** corpses and chariots
18. **(A)** Alcibiades
19. **(D)** lion cub
20. **(B)** cleverness
21. **(D)** He is enraged
22. **(A)** A meal
23. **(C)** Socrates
24. **(D)** good sense
25. **(B)** Sophocles

The Frogs Bibliography

Kristen Osborne-Bartucca, author of ClassicNote. Completed on August 14, 2014, copyright held by GradeSaver.

Updated and revised by Aaron Suduiko May 22, 2015. Copyright held by GradeSaver.

Aristophanes. Frogs. Newbury: Focus Publishing, 2008.

Moorton, Richard F. Jr., "Rites of Passage in Aristophanes' 'Frogs'," *The Classical Journal*, Vol. 84, No. 4 (Apr. - May, 1989), pp. 308-324.

James Redfield, "Comedy, Tragedy, and Politics in Aristophanes' 'Frogs'," *Chicago Review*, Vol. 15, No. 4 (Summer - Autumn, 1962), pp. 107-121

Henderson, Jeffrey. "Introduction," in Aristophanes, *Frogs*. Newbury:MA, 2008.

John E. Thorburn, Jr. "Aristophanes." Facts on File Companion to Classical Drama. 2014-08-05. <http://www.fofweb.com/>.

John E. Thorburn, Jr. "The Frogs." Facts on File Companion to Classical Drama. 2014-08-02. <http://www.fofweb.com/>.

Bloom, Harold. "The Frogs." Aristophanes, Bloom's Major Dramatists. 2014-08-01. <http://www.fofweb.com/>.

Cook, James Wyatt. "The Frogs." Encyclopedia of Ancient Literature. 2014-08-03. <http://www.fofweb.com/>.

Concannon, Kate. "The Frogs." Facts on File: Encyclopedia of Themes in Literature. 2014-08-04. <http://www.fofweb.com/>.

Hubbard, Thomas. "The Frogs in Greek Literature." Aristophanes, Bloom's Major Dramatists. 2014-08-01. <http://www.fofweb.com/>.

Concannon, Kate. "ambition in The Frogs." Facts on File: Encyclopedia of Themes in Literature. 2014-08-01. <http://www.fofweb.com/>.

Concannon, Kate. "identity in The Frogs." Facts on File: Encyclopedia of Themes in Literature. 2014-08-01. <http://www.fofweb.com/>.

Printed in Great Britain
by Amazon

54142699R00050